FAMILY RECIPES

*Favorite Recipes of
Lori Bard,
Sharon Russell, and
Peggy Bard*

Lori Bard

Family

Recipes

ISBN # 9798713882624

Date of Publication: April, 2020

TABLE OF CONTENTS

TO THE CHEF

Hi there! I am a 60 year old woman, and this book is a collection of great recipes and my legacy.

When one of my sisters got married about 40+ years ago, I typed up all of my mom's recipes, organized the recipes by their dish type, and put them in a three ring binder as a wedding gift to my sister. My mom's recipes included recipes from cooking classes she'd attended, recipes handwritten on index cards from friends and relatives, recipes cut out from magazines and recipes in her head. Truth be told, after all this work I decided to "gift" myself and the rest of the family in addition to my bride sister. I made three copies of each hand typed recipe, put each page in a three hole punched plastic pocket, and put each set of recipes in a three ring binder. My sister's wedding gift also became a gift to my other sister, myself and my mom!

Recently, I looked at my collection of recipes. I still my three ring binder that was a copy of the wedding gift to my sister 40+ years ago. I have recipes written on index cards. I have printouts of recipes I got on the internet. I have printouts of recipes I got through email. I have recipes on torn out pages from magazines. I have a huge pile of recipes.

I decided to go through my recipes and put the recipes that I think are the most delicious and most meaningful in this book. The original intent of the book was to pass the recipes down to my daughters. So, you'll see personal little notes under a lot of the recipe names. You'll see the recipe for making rhubarb pies which my grandma (Great Grandma Russell) used to make with rhubarb from her garden. You'll see a recipe for meat loaf from back when my Mom (Grandma Sharon) was cooking my dinners. You'll see a recipe for a party batch of Cosmopolitans from ladies get togethers when I was in my 40s. You'll see my favorite dinner party recipes. You'll see my favorite recipes to make for families with a Mom who can use some help with dinner. And, as my family grew up and turned into vegetarians, you'll see some more recent vegetarian recipes. And, since all of us have a sweet tooth. the book is heavy in desserts. A lot of our family time is spent over the holidays, so I included a section of our very best holiday recipes. Some of the longstanding holiday recipes have been replaced over time. Cranberry sauce used to be bought out of a can, and now cranberry sauce is made from fresh ingredients. Sweet potatoes used to be topped with marshmallows, and now they are topped with oats. But, my mom's stuffing recipe has withstood the test of time. And, I added two of the favorite recipes of my mother-in-law, Grandma Peggy.

Now I've got a cookbook that I'm proud to share with you and my daughters, Michelle and Melissa. I hope you enjoy the recipes.

Best,
Lori

PS: Feel free to share your photos and they may just appear in the next edition. Email to lori.r.bard@gmail.com.

BRUNCH

Grandma Peggy's Noodle Pudding

GRANDMA PEGGY'S NOODLE PUDDING

This recipe is compliments of Grandma Peggy. It's also called "Noodle Kugel".My notes are in italics and the real recipe isn't.

INGREDIENTS:

1lb. broad (1/4 inch wide) egg noodles, cooked and drained (*Option: 12 - 16 oz, 1/4 inch - 1 inch wide*)
16 ozs. sour cream
16 ozs. cottage cheese
6 eggs beaten
1 stick melted butter
1 cup peeled and chopped apples
1 cup raisins
1 cup sugar (I think it tastes good with *1/2 cup sugar too*)
1 tsp. Salt
2 tsp. Cinnamon

INSTRUCTIONS:

Mix all ingredients together, pour into greased 9 x 12 baking dish, and bake for one hour in a 325 degree oven. Serve warm or cold, cut into squares.
This is a great Brunch dish.

APPETIZERS

Artichoke Dip
(with crackers and bread for dipping)

ARTICHOKE DIP

This is a recipe that I've had for years. It's really good if you buy a circular loaf of bread, cut out the middle of the loaf (and cut the bread cutout from the middle into bitesize pieces to be dipped into the dip) and put the dip in the area where the loaf was cut out. You may need some crackers in addition to the bread for dipping.

INGREDIENTS:

1 Loaf of freshly made bread in a circular shape and/or crackers
1 cup mayonnaise
2 jars or cans (each about 12 oz) of artichoke hearts
1 cup grated fresh parmesan cheese

INSTRUCTIONS:

Drain the jar of artichokes. Cut the artichoke hearts up into small pieces. Mix all the ingredients together and heat until the cheese melts. Serve this with bread cut out of the loaf you're serving the dip in or crackers.

BLACK BEAN AND CORN SALSA

This is the favorite recipe of my ladies cycling group. We call ourselves the Peninsula Princesses.

INGREDIENTS:

1-2 ears of fresh (uncooked) corn, cut off of the cob (may also substitute with 10 oz. canned corn
1 10 oz. can black beans (drain and rinse well)
1 tomato, diced
2 green onions, chopped
1/4 cup olive oil
1/8 cup balsamic
1 tsp. Tabasco
1 chopped avocado
Cilantro to taste (1/2 - 1 cup of it), cut it or chop it up.
Tortilla Chips or Frito Scoops

INSTRUCTIONS:

Marinate the ingredients up to and including the Tabasco sauce for at least one hour. Before serving, add the avocado and cilantro and mix together. Serve the dip with chips or Fritos for a yummy appetizer.

Broiled Tomatoes and Goat Cheese

BROILED TOMATOES AND GOAT CHEESE

This is a new recipe that I just got in 2020 with many thanks to Morgan Raleigh, a long time friend of my family. This is an absolutely delicious appetizer and gorgeous too.

INGREDIENTS:

1 medium Shallot, diced
4-5 small Tomatoes (Kumato or Roma), sliced 1 inch thick
1 medium sized shallot, diced
Handful of Cherry Tomatoes, halved
Handful of Green Grapes, halved
Small Shallot (or 1/2 of a large shallot), diced
1/4 cup Dry White Wine
2 cloves of garlic, chopped
4-5 sprigs of Fresh Thyme
1 tsp. Dried oregano
1 Tbsp. fresh, lightly chopped Oregano
Dash of Chili Flakes
1-2 Tbsp. Fresh Basil, chopped
Wheel of Goat Cheese (or Buratta…but, do not broil burette), close to 4 oz.

INSTRUCTIONS:

Put about 2 Tbsp of olive oil in an oven safe frying pan (a cast iron pan would be perfect) and heat to medium high. Add the diced shallot, sliced tomatoes and garlic. Add in a few sprigs of thyme and a dash of chili flakes and salt. Cook, but don't stir, until the tomatoes are browned.

Flip the tomatoes and sprinkle with dried oregano and some garlic powder. Pour in the white wine and loosen the brown bits from the bottom of the pan. Let the mixture simmer until soupy, about 10 minutes.

Add the halved cherry tomatoes and halved grapes to the mixture. Make a whole in the center of the pan and place the wheel of cheese in the middle.

Put the oven on Broil. Put the mixture in the oven until the cheese is golden, about 5 minutes. Remove the mixture from the oven. You can take out the thyme sprigs, if you'd like at this point.

Sprinkle the mixture with fresh oregano, basil, sea salt and black pepper. Keep the mixture in the pan which will be used as the "dip" pan. Serve with crunchy bread or crackers.

SOUPS

FRENCH ONION SOUP

This is Grandma Sharon's Recipe.

INGREDIENTS:

1/2 stick Butter (1 1/2 sticks total for the entire recipe)
2 lbs. sliced Onions (about 1 dozen or 8 cups of onions)
2 cloves crushed Garlic
1 Bay Leaf
8 cups of Stock (the recipe calls for Beef or chicken stock, but you can use Vegetable stock)
1/2 cup white wine (like a dry Sauterne) or Sherry
Salt, Pepper and Accent (Grandma Sharon used Accent. I skip the Accent)
1 Tbsp. Worchester
1 loaf of French or Italian bread (stale is fine)
1 stick of butter, melted
1 cup grated Parmesan cheese

INSTRUCTIONS:

Put the butter in a 6-8 qt. pan. Put the heat on medium to medium-high. Add the sliced onions, crushed garlic and bay leaf to the pan and saute until lightly brown. Stir this occasionally. Once the mixture is browned, add the stock, wine, seasonings, and bring the mixture to a boil. Cover and simmer for 30 minutes. You can freeze at this point, if you want to.

* * *

Cut the bread into 1/2 inch slices. Make sure the slices of bread will fit into the soup cups. Lay the slices of bread on a pan when the correct size is obtained and broil until the slices are brown on the top. Remove the bread from the oven.

Dip the unbrowned side of the bread into melted butter and into cheese. Put the bread back into the broiler and cook until the cheese is browned.

Put the soup in the bowl and then top with the browned bread and enjoy!

This should make 12-14 cups of French Onion Soup.

CLASSIC FRENCH ONION SOUP

I found this recipe in "Fine Cooking" in late 2019. It's a great recipe for French Onion Soup. French Onion Soup has been a favorite of our family's for as long as I can remember..back the days we'd have dinner at Bucks in Woodside after horseback riding lessons.

INGREDIENTS:

2 oz. (1/4 cup) unsalted butter, more for the baking sheet
4 medium-large yellow onions (about 2 lb.), thinly sliced (8 cups)
Kosher salt and freshly ground black pepper
1 tsp. granulated sugar
1 small baguette (1/2 lb.), cut into 1/2-inch slices
2 quarts roasted beef broth or lower-salt canned beef or chicken broth OR VEGETABLE BROTH
1 bay leaf
2 cups grated Gruyère

INSTRUCTIONS:

Melt the butter in a 4-quart pot over medium heat. Stir in the onions and season with 1 tsp. salt and a few grinds of pepper. Reduce the heat to low. Press a piece of foil onto the onions to cover them completely, cover the pot with a lid, and cook, stirring occasionally (you will have to lift the foil), until the onions are very soft but not falling apart, 40 to 50 minutes. Remove the lid and foil, raise the heat to medium high, and stir in the sugar. Cook, stirring often, until very deeply browned, 10 to 15 minutes.

Meanwhile, to make the croûtes (baguette toasts), position a rack in the center of the oven and heat the oven to 350°F. Butter a rimmed baking sheet and arrange the baguette slices on the sheet in a single layer. Bake until the bread is crisp and lightly browned, turning once, 15 to 20 minutes. Set aside.

Add the broth and bay leaf to the caramelized onions and bring the soup to a boil over medium-high heat. Reduce the heat to medium low and simmer for 10 minutes to blend the flavors. Discard the bay leaf and season to taste with salt and pepper.

To serve, position a rack 6 inches from the broiler and heat the broiler to high. Put 6 to 8 broilerproof soup bowls or crocks on a baking sheet. Put 2 or 3 croûtes in each bowl and ladle the hot soup on top. Sprinkle with the cheese and broil until the top is browned and bubbly, 2 to 5 minutes. Serve immediately.

Make Ahead Tips
The soup and croûtes can be made up to 2 days ahead. Store the soup in the refrigerator and the croûtes in an airtight container at room temperature.

This recipe will serve 6-8

Pasta Fagioli
(This one is made with "Beef-Less" Beef)

PASTA FAGIOLI

This is a really good recipe from Grandma Sharon.

INGREDIENTS:

1 onion, chopped
2 cloves garlic, chopped
Optional (1/2 lb. hamburger or sausage or another protein, chopped)

20 oz. can of beans, cannellini beans are the best, but kidney beans can be used too. Include the liquid (well, the directions say this but I don't know if I use the liquid)
20 oz. stock (she suggests chicken or beef, but you can use vegetable)
8 oz. tomato sauce (from the can)
Salt, pepper and Accent (don't worry about the "Accent"..trendy at the time)
1 tsp. oregano
1 Tbsp. basil
1 cup uncooked pasta, any kind (not lasagna noodles though!)
Handful of chopped parsley
Parmesan cheese
French or Italian bread
Ricotta cheese (optional)

INSTRUCTIONS:

Saute the onion, garlic, and meat (optional) in about 1/4 cup olive oil for 5-10 minutes in a big soup pot on medium high heat. Salt and pepper the mixture when you start to cook it.

Add the beans, stock, tomato sauce, oregano and basil to the soup pot. Add salt and pepper. Bring to a boil. Cover. Simmer for 15-20 minutes.

Cook the pasta in another pot for the minimum amount of time in the instructions on the pasta box. Drain it when it's done and run cold water over the pasta in the draining bowl to keep it from cooking anymore.

When ready to serve, bring bean mixture to a boil. Add the drained pasta. Allow the soup to heat and serve. Garnish with parsley. Serve with Parmesan Cheese and French or Italian bread You can also offer ricotta cheese to let people add to their soup.

This recipe makes for 6-8 bowls or 12-14 cups of soup.

SALADS

Beet Salad

BEET SALAD

I cannot remember who I got this recipe from but it's yummy!

INGREDIENTS:

4-5 Beets, medium sized, cooked (see note below), peeled and cut into about 1 inch squares (or, you could use a package of precooked propelled beets)
3 - 4 oz. Goat Cheese, broken up into something close to 1/4 inch pieces
Balsamic Vinegar (Peach flavored balsamic vinegar is the best!), about 1/8 cup
Extra Virgin Olive Oil, about 1/4 cup
Cilantro, or another herb, cleaned, cut up into small pieces to measure about 1-2 Tbsp.

INSTRUCTIONS:

Mix the ingredients together right before serving. You can add more cheese, olive oil or balsamic vinegar if you think the salad will taste better. Serve and enjoy!

You may optionally add candied walnuts, to make it even better.

Note:If you have fresh beets, cut off most of the stem (leave 1/2 - 1 inch of the green stem on) and put the beets (skin and all) in a pot of boiling water. Boil them until you can put a fork in them easily (fork tender). Dain the water out, let the beets cool, and then peel off the beet skin.

**Caesar Salad
(this one is made without croutons)**

CAESAR SALAD

I got this recipe from Grandma Sharon. It makes up a delicious Caesar salad!

INGREDIENTS:

1 clove of garlic
1 can of mashed anchovies, fluid drained out
1 tsp. Worcestershire
1 tsp. dijon mustard
1/2 of a lemon, juice only
1/8 cup of red wine vinegar
1/4 cup of olive oil
1 beaten egg
1-2 Heads of romaine, washed and torn into pieces
Grated Parmesan cheese
Croutons (optional)

INSTRUCTIONS:

Mix the ingredients through the egg. I mix it all in the blender.
Pour the mixture over the romaine. Toss will grated Parmesan cheese. Add croutons, if desired.

Warm Cauliflower and Herbed Barley Salad

WARM CAULIFLOWER AND HERBED BARLEY SALAD

This is a Bon Appetit recipe which I found years ago. Michelle and Melissa always really liked this salad. This recipe is for 4 servings.

INGREDIENTS:

1/2 cup pearled barley
Kosher salt
1 tablespoon finely grated lemon zest
3 tablespoons fresh lemon juice
1 tablespoon mayonnaise
1 teaspoon Dijon mustard
6 tablespoons olive oil, divided
Freshly ground black pepper
1 head cauliflower, cut into florets
1 15-ounce can gigante, corona, or butter beans, rinsed
1/2 cup flat-leaf parsley leaves, divided
2 tablespoons fresh tarragon leaves, divided

INSTRUCTIONS:

Place barley in a large saucepan; add water to cover by 2 inches. Season with salt. Bring to a boil and cook until tender, 25-30 minutes. Drain; run under cold water. Set aside.

Meanwhile, whisk lemon juice, mayonnaise, Dijon mustard, and 5 tablespoons oil in a medium bowl until emulsified. Season dressing with salt and pepper; set aside.

Heat remaining 1 tablespoon oil in a large skillet over medium heat. Add cauliflower; cook, turning occasionally, until browned in spots, 10-12 minutes. Add 2 tablespoons water, cover, and cook until just tender, about 2 minutes longer. Season with salt and pepper.

Transfer cauliflower to a large bowl; add beans, 1/4 cup parsley, 1 tablespoon tarragon, reserved barley, and half of reserved dressing. Toss to coat; season with salt and pepper.

Divide salad among bowls; drizzle remaining dressing over. Garnish with lemon zest, 1/4 cup parsley, and 1 tablespoon tarragon.

Hot German Potato Salad

HOT GERMAN POTATO SALAD

This is a salad that I love. The recipe is compliments of Grandma Sharon.

INGREDIENTS:

6 baking potatoes (boiled so that a fork can be inserted into them and they are not cracked apart), and cut into bitesize pieces while still warm (skins left on)
6 slices of bacon, cooked and cut into bitesize pieces
3/4 cup diced onion
2 Tbsp. flour
1 1/2 tsp. salt
1-2 Tbsp. sugar
1/2 tsp. celery seed
Pepper, to taste
3/4 cup water
1/3 cup vinegar (distilled white or apple cider)

INSTRUCTIONS:

Boil the water and vinegar and add the other ingredients (except the potatoes and bacon). Pour this mixture over the potatoes and bacon and gently toss.

Potato Salad

POTATO SALAD

This is a great recipe to make with your leftover hardboiled eggs from Easter.

INGREDIENTS:

4-5 baking potatoes, boiled until they start cracking, drained from the water, cooled, peeled (easy to do after the potatoes are cooked) and cut into about 1/2 inch squarish pieces
2-3 hard boiled eggs, chilled, cut up into small pieces
Green Onions, about 6, chopped into small pieces
Mayonnaise to taste (about 1/2 cup)
Salt to Taste

INSTRUCTIONS:

Put the potatoes, eggs and green onions in a bowl. Add mayonnaise and a generous amount of salt. Mix up. If you need more, add more mayonnaise and salt. Let the salad chill for a bit before serving. And, salt it again before serving. (I don't know where the salt goes, but it needs more salt before serving).

**Spinach Salad
(This one is made with Vegetarian
"Bacon")**

SPINACH SALAD

This is from Grandma Sharon's Recipe book. It's a great tasting salad. This recipe includes enough dressing for four salads.

INGREDIENTS:

1 package of spinach leaves, washed and torn into bitesize pieces
6 strips of bacon (or a vegetarian equivalent), fry the bacon until crunchy and put it on a paper towel to get off the oil
Fresh mushrooms (optional), cleaned and sliced

Dressing for 4 Salads:
1 cup olive oil
1/2 cup red wine vinegar
1/2 cup sugar
1/3 cup ketchup
1 dash of salt (a dash is equal to 1/8 tsp)

INSTRUCTIONS:

Blend the oil, vinegar, sugar, ketchup and salt well. Refrigerate. (You can put the fresh mushrooms in this mixture to marinate if you want). When you're ready to serve, toss the spinach, bacon and 1/4 the dressing together.

VEGETABLE SIDES

ACORN SQUASH

This is a totally delicious recipe from Grandma Sharon.

INGREDIENTS:

1/2 an acorn squash/person
2 Tbsp. Unsalted Butter/ person
2-5 Tbsp. Brown Sugar/person

INSTRUCTIONS:

Preheat the oven to 350 degrees. Cut the squash in half (be careful!) and scrape out the seeds.

Place the squash with the middle down, on a greased or sprayed baking sheet. Bake the squash for 30 minutes. Take the squash out of the oven and turn it right side up. Fill the center with the butter and brown sugar. Put it back in the oven for 15-30 minutes (until the squash is soft when you prick it with a fork) and then serve. Yummy!!!

GREEN BEAN ALMONDINE

This is a recipe from Grandma Sharon. I think it's super tasty.

INGREDIENTS:

2 package of frozen French string beans (I use 2 lbs fresh French string beans…wash them, cut them in about 1-2 inch pieces)
1 stick of butter
1 cup sliced almonds (can go down to 4 oz)

INSTRUCTIONS:

Add the string beans to about 4 cups of boiling water with a pinch of salt. Boil for 5-7 minutes. Strain the water out and let the beans cool a bit. (Or, steam fresh French string beans until they turn dark green, then, put the pan in the sink, put ice over them (to preserve the pretty green and stop them from overcooking).

Saute the sliced almonds in the butter (I'd use medium heat). Saute until the almonds are lightly browned.

Place the drained, cooked beans in the almond mixture. Salt, pepper and accent the mixture. Toss. Serve.

MAIN DISHES

CHICKEN AND DUMPLINGS

This used to be my one of my favorite meals! I got sick the day after I had it once and it lost the magical spell it had on me. This recipe is from Grandma Sharon.

INGREDIENTS:

Whole chicken
Chicken bouillon (or chicken stock)
Parsley (optional)
Accent (optional…a "dated" ingredient not used much anymore)
Bay Leaves (2)
2 cups Bisquick
1/2 cup milk

INSTRUCTIONS:

Put the chicken in a large pot. You can cut off the legs and wings or put the whole chicken in the pot. Cover with water. Add a couple of chicken bouillon cubes, salt, pepper, accent, parsley and a couple of bay leaves. Bring the pot to a boil and cook on low for a couple of hours Take the chicken out and debone. Put the chicken meat back in the pot to make the stew.

Mix the Bisquick and milk until a soft dough forms.

Do NOT overmix. Let the dough set for a few minutes so it starts to rise. Drop the dough by spoonfuls onto stew (do not drop directly into liquid). Cook uncovered over low heat for 10 minutes. Cover and cook 10 minutes longer.

Chicken Marbella
(with Vegetarian "Chicken")

Chicken Marbella

CHICKEN MARBELLA

I love making this recipe for dinner parties or when making dinner for someone who is sick. It's a recipe from Silver Palate. I just use chicken breasts or chicken-less chicken instead of the entire chicken. It's great served with couscous.

INGREDIENTS:

1/2 cup olive oil
1/2 cup red wine vinegar
1 cup pitted prunes
1/2 cup pitted Spanish green olives
1/2 cup capers with a bit of juice
6 bay leaves
1 head of garlic, peeled and finely pureed
1/4 cup dried oregano
Coarse salt and freshly ground black pepper, to taste
10 chicken breasts, or a vegetarian chicken substitute
1 cup brown sugar
1 cup dry white wine
1/4 cup fresh Italian (flat-leaf) parsley or fresh cilantro, finely chopped

INSTRUCTIONS:

Combine the olive oil, vinegar, prunes, olives, capers and juice, bay leaves, garlic, oregano, and salt and pepper in a large bowl. Add the chicken and stir to coat. Cover the bowl and refrigerate overnight.

Preheat the oven to 350°F.

Arrange the chicken in a single layer in one or two large, shallow baking pans and spoon the marinade over it evenly. Sprinkle the chicken pieces with the brown sugar and pour the white wine around them.

Bake until the chicken is just done, usually 50 minutes to 1 hour. Turn the chicken over about halfway through the baking cycle.

With a slotted spoon, transfer the chicken, prunes, olives, and capers to a serving platter. Moisten with a few spoonfuls of the pan juices and sprinkle generously with the parsley or cilantro. Pass the remaining pan juices in a sauceboat.

This will serve about 10 people.

Coq-Au-Vin
(with Vegetarian "Chicken", Baby Bella Mushrooms, Fresh Pearl Onions, and Edamame Noodles)

* * *

COQ-AU-VIN

This is a recipe from Grandma Sharon. It makes a delicious meal that was a favorite of everyone in our house. I've added notes for making the vegan equivalent.

INGREDIENTS:
Chicken (or Chicken Substitute) for four people
1/4 lb salt pork, diced, (OR about 3 Tbsp Olive Oil)
2 cloves of garlic, crushed
1 bay leaf
2 Handfulls of parsley, chopped…use 1/2 in the pot and 1/2 for garnish when the meal is prepared
1 8oz can of mushroom heads, drained (or, feel free to use fresh mushrooms)
1/2 cup red wine
1/2 cup tomato sauce
2 cups chicken stock (or Vegetable stock)
Salt, pepper and Accent (I skip the Accent but it is Grandma's recipe)
1/4 tsp. Oregano
1/4 tsp. Thyme
1/4 tsp. Majoram
1/4 tsp. Tarragon
1 tsp Kitchen Bouquet, for color (I skip this)
9 drops of red food coloring (optional, and I skip this)
1 lb. jar of pearl onions, washed and drained (If you can't find a jar, just buy fresh pearl onions, cut

off one end of each, boil them for 2 minutes, then take the "skin" off after they've cooled off)
2 Tbsp. Dissolved cornstarch, in hot water (Go ahead and skip this if you don't mind a more liquid sauce)
1 lb. Pasta

INSTRUCTIONS:

Cut chicken in small pieces. Place the salt pork or olive oil in a 10-12 inch pot. Add the chicken or chicken substitute and cook for 5 minutes on medium high heat. Add onion, garlic, bay leaf, 1/2 the parsley and mushrooms and cook for 5 minutes on medium high heat. Add wine, tomato sauce, chicken (or vegetable) stock, and seasonings. Bring to boil. Cover. Simmer or 25-30 minutes, until chicken or chicken substitute is tender. Add the pearl onions. Thicken the sauce with cornstarch. Bring the mixture back to a boil and simmer for 5 minutes. Serve garnished with parsley.
Cook the noodles according to the package instructions and drain the water from the noodles. Put the Coq-Au-Vin over the cooked noodles and enjoy your dish!
Note:The Coq-Au-Viin be made in advance, just bring to a boil before serving.

MEAT LOAF

This is Grandma Sharon's recipe and it's delicious, if you don't eat meat, use a plant based ground beefless beef.

INGREDIENTS:

1 lb Ground round beef (or a Plant Based Ground Beef alternative)
1 Onion, chopped
1 1/2 tsp garlic salt
1 1/2 cup Bread Crumbs
1 Egg
1-2 Tbsp. dry mustard, depending on how spicy you like it
2 Tbsp. brown sugar
2/3 cup Ketchup

INSTRUCTIONS:

Mix *(I mix it with my clean hands)* the ground round, chopped onion, garlic salt, breadcrumbs and egg. Add salt and pepper. Put the mixture in a loaf pan. Blend the Ketchup, Dry mustard and Brown Sugar to make the topping. Put the topping on top of the mixture. Bake for 1 hour at 350 degrees.

SALMON MARINADE

This is a pretty darn good marinade for salmon. A friend of mine named Amy shared this recipe with me.

INGREDIENTS:

1 salmon fillet (2 lbs for 4 people)
1/2 cup soy sauce
1/4 cup honey
1/4 cup orange juice
4 cloves minced garlic
1 tsp. ground ginger
1/4 tsp. red pepper flakes

INSTRUCTIONS:

Remove any bones from the salmon fillet and place the fillet in a gallon sized resealable bag. In a small bowl, whisk together the soy sauce, honey, orange juice, garlic, ginger and pepper flakes. Pour this in the bag with the salmon. Refrigerate and let marinate for 30 minutes.

Cook the salmon over a grill, in a large skillet, or bake. If you bake, preheat the oven to 375 degrees F. Grease the baking sheet (olive oil or cooking spray) so the salmon doesn't stick to it. Bake in the preheated oven for 15-20 minutes, or until the salmon flakes easily with a fork.

SPICED FILLET OF BEEF WITH MIZUNA SALAD

This was my go to recipe for dinner with friends for many a year. It's delicious!

INGREDIENTS:

For beef
2 teaspoons whole black peppercorns
2 1/2 teaspoons cumin seeds
2 1/2 teaspoons coriander seeds
2 teaspoons dried hot red pepper flakes
4 teaspoons kosher salt
3 1/2 pounds center-cut beef tenderloin roast (fillet of beef), trimmed and, if necessary, tied
2 tablespoons vegetable oil
For salad
1 tablespoon extra-virgin olive oil
1 1/2 teaspoons fresh lemon juice
1 teaspoon minced shallot
1/4 teaspoon salt
4 ounces mizuna or baby arugula, trimmed

INSTRUCTIONS:

For beef: Preheat oven to 425°F.
Toast peppercorns, cumin and coriander. Then, cool completely. Grind spices with red pepper flakes in an electric coffee/spice grinder or with a mortar and pestle. Stir in kosher salt.

* * *

Pat beef dry and sprinkle with spices on all sides, pressing to adhere. Heat oil in a large flameproof roasting pan set across 2 burners over high heat until just smoking, then brown beef on all sides, about 2 minutes.

Roast in middle of oven until an instant-read thermometer inserted diagonally 2 inches into center registers 120°F, about 25 minutes. Let beef stand in pan 25 minutes. Beef will continue to cook as it stands, reaching 130°F (medium-rare).

Make salad and slice beef: Whisk together oil, lemon juice, shallot, and salt in a bowl, then add pepper to taste.

Untie beef if necessary, then slice. Toss mizuna with dressing and serve beef topped with salad.

This makes about 6 servings.

DESSERTS

FLAMING DESSERTS

Bananas Foster

BANANAS FOSTER

This is a really yummy dessert recipe compliments of Grandma Sharon. This recipe will serve 6-8.

INGREDIENTS:

1 stick of butter
1/2 cup white sugar
1/2 cup brown sugar
1 tsp. cinnamon
4 bananas, peeled and halved
1 cup rum (80 to 90 proof, NOT 151 Rum)
Vanilla ice cream
Almonds (optional)
2 oz banana liqueur (optional)

INSTRUCTIONS:

Add the butter, sugars, and cinnamon together. Cook on medium high to high heat for 5 minutes or so, until it looks like a glaze. You can prepare this earlier and save it until evening.

Put the glaze back on the fire (if you took it off the fire and saved it). Add bananas. Turn the bananas until they are coated with the glaze.

Dish a bit of ice cream in each dessert dish.

Add cup of rum to the glaze and banana mixture and have the burner on high heat. Allow the rum to reduce/get warm for 1-2 minutes. Flame the mixture. This is the fun part! Use a lighter to light the contents of the frying pan. The whole pan will go on fire (it's fine). Use a spoon to keep mixing up the dessert and burn the rum off. When the fire is done, you can add sliced almonds and/or 2 oz of banana liquor.

Put the bananas on top of or next to the ice cream and pour the sauce over the ice cream and bananas.

CHERRIES JUBILEE

This is a recipe that Grandma Sharon used to make when we had a special dinner. I make it for dessert at special dinners too. It's delicious and the flambe part is fun!

INGREDIENTS:

1 can of pitted sweet cherries
1 pt of vanilla ice cream
1/2 cup sugar
1/4 tsp. Lemon extract
1/4 tsp. Orange extract
1/4 cup orange marmalade (or another good preservative is fine and delicious)
Liquor (brandy is good, vodka works too!)
1 Tbsp cornstarch

INSTRUCTIONS:

In a skillet, place the juice of the cherries, sugar, lemon extract, orange extract and orange marmalade. Bring the mixture to a boil. If you'd like, you can thicken the mixture with 1 Tbsp. Cornstarch dissolved with 1 Tbsp of wine or liquor. Allow the mixture to boil for about 5 minutes or until it is thick. Turn off the heat. Add the cherries. You can make this part of the recipe earlier, if you want.

When ready to serve, bring the mixture back to a

boil (if you made it earlier). Put a scoop of ice cream in each bowl.

Flame the sauce by warming a spoon over the boiling sauce. Place 1-2 oz of liquor into the spoon. Make sure to move the bottle of alcohol away from the skillet! Sprinkle a tsp. of sugar over the entire mixture. Light the alcohol in the spoon and let the liquid drizzle down and make a pretty fire on the mixture. Put the cherries and sauce over the ice cream when the flame has gone out.

Serves 4-6 people.

CAKES AND PIES

Patty's Blueberry Crumble
(with whipped cream on top)

PATTY'S BLUEBERRY CRUMBLE

This recipe is from my friend, Patty Raleigh. It's a keeper!

INGREDIENTS:

Topping:
3/4 cup all purpose flour
3/4 cup old-fashioned oats
1/2 cup (packed) golden brown sugar
1/2 tsp. ground cinnamon
1/4 tsp. fine sea salt
1/2 cup (1 stick) unsalted butter, directly out of the refrigerator, cut into 1/2 inch cubes (*or cut on the lines for Tbsp on the butter packing*)
3/4 cup chopped walnuts (about 3 1/2 ounces)

Filling:
3/4 cup sugar
2 Tbsp. cornstarch
1/4 tsp. ground cinnamon
6 cups blueberries, washed

Vanilla Ice Cream or Whipped Cream

INSTRUCTIONS:

For Topping:
Mix the flour, oats, brown sugar, cinnamon and

salt in a medium bowl. Add butter and rub in with fingertips until mixture comes together in moist clumps. Stir in walnuts.

For Filling:
Position rack in center of oven and preheat to 350 degrees F. Mix sugar, cornstarch, cinnamon and salt in a large bowl. Add the blueberries and toss to coat. Transfer blueberry mixture to 11x7x2 inch greased (with butter or cooking oil spray) glass baking dish. Sprinkle topping over.
Bake crisp until filling is bubbling around edges and topping is crisp and golden, about 1 hour. Cool at least 20 minutes. Serve warm with ice cream or whip cream.

This makes 6-8 servings.

GERMAN CHOCOLATE PIE

*This was made for Aunt Ruth's Rehearsal Dinner
in our backyard deck*

INGREDIENTS:

2 cups sugar
6 Tbsp. cocoa
3 eggs
1 tsp. vanilla
1/2 cup melted butter
Pinch of salt
2 cups flaked coconut
1 cup chopped nuts
13 oz. evaporated milk
2 pie shells (in the frozen section)

INSTRUCTIONS:

Mix dry ingredients except coconut. Add Eggs.
Blend. Add butter and milk. Add coconut and nuts.
Pour into 2 deep dish pie shells.

Bake 50 minutes at 350 degrees.

RHUBARB PIE

This recipe came from my Grandma Crockett, Michelle' and Melissa's Great Grandma and my mom's mom. Her first name was Naomi, and she was called Nan. It has always been a family summer dessert favorite.

INGREDIENTS:

The crust:
2 cups flour
1/2 tsp. baking powder
1/4 cup sugar
3/4 cup shortening (I know, it sounds gross, but is delicious in this recipe!)
1 1/2 Tbsp. milk (can add an extra 1/2 Tbsp. if you want)
Pinch of salt

The filling:
3 cups rhubarb, cleaned and sliced
1 1/2 cups sugar
2 beaten eggs
1/8 cup milk

The frosting:
Powdered sugar (about 1/2 cup)
Milk (enough to make the powdered sugar liquid enough to put on pie)

INSTRUCTIONS:

Mix together the crust ingredients. Pat the ingredients into a 9" x 10" pan that has been greased.

Mix together the filling ingredients and spread over the dough in the pan. Bake at 400 degrees for 25-35 minutes.

When baked, remove and frost with a thin frosting of powdered sugar and milk.

Steve Gitelman's Strawberry Pie (Recipe written out especially for me!)

STEVE GITELMAN'S STRAWBERRY PIE

This Recipe was given to us by Steve Gitelman, a friend of Mom's since 1977 (he dated her college roommate). The recipe comes from the wife of the president of UNC (don't remember which one or which year!).

INGREDIENTS:

1 qt Fresh Strawberries (32 oz)
1 cup Sugar
3 Tbsp. Corn Starch
Dash Salt
9 inch baked Pie Shell
1 cup Sweetened Whip Cream

INSTRUCTIONS:

Bake the pie shell (I use a frozen pie shell that I bake according to the instructions on the container.).

Refrigerate 1/2 of the strawberries. Crush the rest of the strawberries. Bring the crushed strawberries to a boil.

Combine the sugar, cornstarch and salt and stir into the hot mixture. Do NOT boil the hot mixture, but let it cook for 10 minutes. Set the mixture aside to cool.

Take the pre baked pie shell out and spread the chilled whole berries (*if they are big berries, cut them into more bitesize pieces)* throughout the pie shell. Put the cooled mixture on top. Refrigerate this pie uncovered.

Serve the pie with whip cream.

CHOCOLATE DOMES

CHOCOLATE DOMES

This is a recipe that I found in the book San Francisco Flavors by the San Francisco Junior League. I found the recipe after I tried chocolate domes cooked by a Duke friend of Steve's wife named Linda. I loved the dessert and asked for the recipe, and she refused to give me the recipe. The only clue she gave is that the good taste is in the quality of the chocolate you use. So, use really really good quality chocolate!

INGREDIENTS:

These ingredients are given based on you buying a Scharfen Berger Bittersweet Chocolate Bar. You can use the amounts in parenthesis if you end up buying another kind of chocolate in different increments.

9.7 oz (1 bar) of Scharfen Berger Bittersweet Chocolate (6oz)
1 1/4 cups unsalted butter (3/4 cup)
5 eggs at room temperature (3 eggs)
5 egg yolks at room temperature (3 eggs)
5/8 cup sugar (6 Tbsp.)
1 1/2 Tbsp.   pure vanilla extract (1 Tbsp.)
3/4 tsp. Salt (1/2 tsp)
1/2 cup flour (5 Tbsp)
Creme fraiche, fresh raspberries, and fresh mint springs for garnish (or a favorite ice cream)

INSTRUCTIONS:

Preheat the oven to 375 degrees. Butter and flour 9 (or 6) 6 ounce custard cups or ramekins. Set aside. In a medium saucepan, melt the chocolate with the butter over low heat. I usually put the chocolate and butter in a pan and then put that pan in water kept hot with the stovetop on medium heat. It'll keep the chocolate from overcooking. Let cool slightly.

In a mixing bowl, combine the eggs, egg yolks, and sugar. Beat until the mixture is pale and a slowly dissolving ribbon forms on the surface when the beaters are lifted, about 10 minutes. Mix in the vanilla and salt. Beat in the flour. Add the chocolate mixture and beat until thick and glossy, about 5 minutes. Pour the batter equally into the cups or ramekins. At this point, the cups or ramekins can be covered with plastic wrap and refrigerated or frozen until later use.

Remove the cups or ramekins from the refrigerator or freezer and place immediately in the preheated oven. Bake until each cake is set around the edges but moves slightly in the center, about 10 minutes, or 15 minutes if frozen; do NOT over bake! Let cool slightly. Invert the cups or ramekins onto plates. Garnish each with a dollop of creme fraiche, fresh rasberries and a mint sprig (or use a yummy ice cream).

COOKIES

Chocolate Chip Cookies

CHOCOLATE CHIP COOKIES

This is actually the Nestle Toll House Cookie recipe with the chocolate chip amount DOUBLED and using HIGH QUALITY MILK chocolate chips instead of the semi-sweet Nestle Chocolate chips that the original recipe recommends. The recipe says it makes 5 dozen, but I usually come out with less (eat some batter occasionally and make big cookies!).

INGREDIENTS:

1 cup (2 sticks) butter, softened…I use unsalted butter
3/4 cup granulated sugar
3/4 cup packed brown sugar
1 teaspoon vanilla extract
2 large eggs
2 12-ounce packages of High Quality MILK Chocolate Chips
2 1/4 cups all-purpose flour
1 teaspoon baking soda
1 teaspoon salt
1 cup chopped nuts (optional…I'd use pecans or walnuts)

INSTRUCTIONS:

PREHEAT oven to 375° F. Beat butter, granulated

sugar, brown sugar and vanilla extract in large mixer bowl until creamy. Add eggs, one at a time, beating well after each addition. Add the salt, baking soda, and flour. Stir in chocolate chips and nuts. Drop by rounded tablespoon (or may be a little bit bigger…may. be two to three tablespoons in size if you like bigger cookies) onto ungreased baking sheets.

BAKE for 9 to 11 minutes or until golden brown. Cool on baking sheets for 2 minutes; remove to wire racks to cool completely.

FOR HIGH ALTITUDE BAKING (5,200 feet or above): Increase flour to 2 1/2 cups. Add 2 teaspoons water with flour. Bake drop cookies for 8 to 10 minutes or until they start to brown.

CHEWY GINGER MOLASSES COOKIES

I started making this recipe December, 2019. I had been searching for a recipe for really yummy ginger molasses cookies for years (since ladies trips to Yellowstone Club where they served the best ginger molasses cookies). I think this recipe fits the bill. These are really good served hot out of the oven.

INGREDIENTS:

1 1/2 cups unsalted butter, softened to room temperature (not melted*)
1 cup granulated (white) sugar
1 cup packed brown sugar
1/2 cup unsulphured molasses
2 eggs
4 1/2 cups all-purpose flour
4 teaspoons baking soda
1 tablespoon ground ginger
2 teaspoons ground cinnamon
1 teaspoon ground cloves
1 teaspoon salt

INSTRUCTIONS:

Using a mixing bowl and mixer (blender), cream together the softened butter and sugars on medium-high speed until the mixture is light and fluffy and a pale yellow color, about 2 minutes, scraping down the sides occasionally as needed. Mix in the eggs (one at a time) and molasses, and beat on medium-low speed until each is combined. Gradually stir in the dry ingredients, first the tablespoonfuls and teaspoonfuls of spices and then the flour until it is all combined.

Transfer the dough to an airtight container and refrigerate for at least 2 hours, or until the dough is completely chilled.

Preheat oven to 350°F. Line a sheet pan with parchment or use the Silplat on a baking dish.

Roll the dough into small balls, about 1-inch in diameter. Fill a separate small bowl with sugar, and roll each ball in the sugar until it is completely coated. Place dough balls on the prepared baking sheet.

Bake for about 8-10 minutes, until the cookies begin to slightly crack on top. (They will crack more while cooling.) Remove from the oven and let cool for 4-5 minutes. Then transfer the cookies to wire racks to cool completely.

RUSSIAN TEACAKES

This is a recipe of Grandma Sharon's. I don't think anyone likes these cookies that melt in your mouth more than I do. They look a bit like snowballs so are good for Christmas. They are also gorgeous and delicious to serve at wedding showers.

INGREDIENTS:

1 cup soft butter (2 sticks), room temperature
1/2 cup sifted confectioners sugar (powdered sugar)
1 tsp vanilla.

2 1/4 cups sifted flour
1/4 tsp. Salt

3/4 cup finely chopped nuts (I use walnuts but pecans would be good too, or almonds)

Confectioners sugar (powdered sugar)….about 1/2 cup, poured in a pan

INSTRUCTIONS:

Mix the butter, powdered sugar and vanilla. Stir in the flour and salt. Mix in the nuts.

Chill the dough (an hour is a good amount of time but more is fine). Preheat the oven to 400 degrees. Roll the dough into 1 inch balls. Place the balls of dough on an ungreased baking sheet (the cookies will not spread so you can put them close to each other). Bake until set, but now brown. Baking time should be 10-12 minutes. While the cookies are still warm, roll them in a pan of powdered sugar. Cool. Roll the cookies in the sugar again.

This recipe should make about 4 dozen cookies.

ALCOHOLIC BEVERAGES

BOAT NIGHT DRINKS

Our friend Ken used to have monthly parties on his boat (while safely in it's slip in the marina). These boats are the signature drinks of Boat Night, and we've decided that we like them enough to drink them off the boat.

INGREDIENTS:

1 1/2 oz. Meyers Rum
1 oz Malibu Coconut Rum
4 oz. Orange, pineapple and banana juice (Dole makes this kind of juice)
Splash of Grenadine (optional)
Maraschino cherry (optional)

INSTRUCTIONS:

Mix all the ingredients together in a tall glass filled with ice. Garnish with the cherry.

BOOTLEGGER

This is a recipe for a delicious summer cocktail. I got the recipe from Jan Dickerson, a good friend who I met when Michelle was a baby.

INGREDIENTS:

12 oz frozen concentrated lemonade (Minute Maid is a good choice)
Mint (clean and take the leaves off the stem)…let's say about 1/4 cup
Sparkling Water
Vodka

INSTRUCTIONS:

Put the frozen concentrated lemonade in a blender with the mint leaves. Turn on the blender and blend. Fill a tall glass with ice. Pour the blended mixture in up until about 1/5 to 1/4 the height of the glass. Add a jigger of vodka. Add sparkling water to fill the glass.

COSMOS FOR A GROUP

I used to make a batch of this for parties. Everyone seems to be able to drink more than one, so make sure and make enough! You can make these way ahead of time and store in the freezer.

INGREDIENTS:

3 Parts Vodka
2 Parts Cranberry Juice (use te sweetened stuff—
if you use the organic fresh juice you'll have to use
some sugar to sweeten)
2 parts Triple Sec
1 part Lime Juice (I use the bottled kind, the
closest you can find to fresh. Fresh would be
better!)
Limes for garnish

INSTRUCTIONS:

Make this up in containers (estimate how much
you'll need for your group's size) and put the
containers in the freezer. About an hour before the
event, take out the very chilled, very delicious fun
drinks and stir it a little until the ice stuff melts
(doesn't take long). Pour the drinks into martini
glasses and serve. Garnish the drinks with a slice
of lime.

As an ingredients example I used 123 oz vodka,

82 oz cranberry juice, 82 oz Triple Sec and 41 oz. Lime Juice....didn't write down how many people it gave a cocktail to, but I'd estimate 40 people, two drinks per person.

EGG NOG

This is a recipe for homemade egg nog. As far as I remember, the recipe came from Grandma Sharon.

INGREDIENTS:

12 eggs, separate the whites and yolks
1 1/2 quarts, whole milk
1 3/4 cups Whiskey
1 1/2 cups Heavy Cream
1 cup Sugar
1/2 cup Jamaican Rum

INSTRUCTIONS:

Beat the egg yolks with the sugar until dissolved. Add liquor, milk and cream. Taste to see if it suits you Then, add stiffly beaten egg whites. Chill in the refrigerator for a couple of hours or more before serving. Sprinkle grated nutmeg on top before serving. This serves about 25.

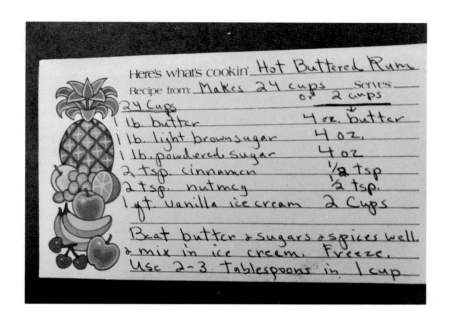

Here's what's cookin' **Hot Buttered Rum**

Recipe from: **Makes 24 cups** Serves

24 Cups   or 2 cups

1 lb. butter   4 oz. butter

1 lb. light brown sugar   4 oz.

1 lb. powdered sugar   4 oz

2 tsp. cinnamon   1/2 tsp

2 tsp. nutmeg   1/2 tsp.

1 qt. vanilla ice cream   2 Cups

Beat butter & sugars & spices well.
& mix in ice cream. Freeze.
Use 2-3 Tablespoons in 1 cup

Hot Buttered Rum
(Grandma Sharon's Index Card)

HOT BUTTERED RUM

This is one of Grandma Sharon's recipes. It's a great warm holiday drink (sorry, but it's loaded with calories!

INGREDIENTS:

To make 24 cups:
1 lb. butter
1 lb. light brown sugar
1 lb. powdered sugar
2 tsp. cinnamon
2 tsp. nutmeg
1 qt vanilla ice cream

INSTRUCTIONS:

Beat the butter and sugars and spices well and mix in the ice cream. Freeze. When ready to drink, put one jigger of rum in cup, put 2-3 Tbsp. of mix in cup and add boiling water. Add 1 jigger of rum to the cup. This is usually served in a coffee cup (if I remember right).

IRISH COFFEE

INGREDIENTS:

Coffee
Whipped Cream
Irish Whiskey

INSTRUCTIONS:

Make coffee the usual way. Pour coffee into Irish coffee glasses or any stemmed 5-6 oz. glasses. Add a jigger of Irish Whiskey to each glass and top with whipped cream.

HEALTHY SNACKS

PUMPKIN CRUNCH

I used to make this and keep it in Tupperware. It's a great healthy snack.

INGREDIENTS:

1 cup pumpkin seeds
1 1/2 tsp. canola oil
2 Tbsp. pure maple syrup
1/2 tsp. cinnamon
1/2 tsp. ground nutmeg
1/2 tsp. ground allspice
1/2 tsp. sea salt
1 1/2 cups dried cranberries

INSTRUCTIONS:

Preheat the oven to 300 degrees. Lightly spray a baking sheet with canola oil.

Toss the pumpkin seeds and canola oil in a small bowl. Spread the coated seeds evenly on the baking sheet. Roast for 20 minutes or until almost dry.

Place the pumpkin seeds in a medium bowl. Add all other ingredients except cranberries and stir.

Return to the baking sheet and roast for 15 minutes or until dry.

* * *

Let the seeds cool and then mix in the cranberries.

This makes 10- 1/2 cup servings. Each serving is 135 calories, 13 grams carbohydrate, 7 grams fat, 4 grams protein, 1 gram fiber

HOLIDAY RECIPES

FRESH CRANBERRY RELISH

This is a recipe I got when I took a Home Chef class in San Francisco. The class was called "Light Holiday Menu". I have served this cranberry relish for years and everyone loves it.

INGREDIENTS:

12 oz. Fresh Cranberries
1 small orange, peel left on, cut into eighths, and with seeds removed
3/4 cup of Super Fine Sugar (it's sold in a carton)
1/2 tsp. Orange Flower Water (in the spice area with all the flavorings)

INSTRUCTIONS:

Chop the cranberries and the orange in a food processor. Stir in the sugar and orange flower water. Let this stand for at lest 30 minutes before serving. 100 calories per serving (serves 8-12 people)

GRANDMA PEGGY'S CRANBERRY/ORANGE SAUCE

This recipe is from Grandma Peggy. Here's what she says: " I got mine many years ago during a cooking class given by a local chef. I took this class with my friend Irene, whose family adored it. When she died, at her memorial service. a niece from New Jersey spoke, and mentioned the famous cranberry sauce, which she said would be passed down in the family and always be a part of their future Thanksgivings!".

INGREDIENTS:

1 lb. Cranberries
1whole Navel Orange
2 cups Sugar
1 cup cold water
Apricot jam
2 Tbsp. lemon juice
1 cup slivered Almonds

INSTRUCTIONS:

Place unpeeled Orange in processor, and chop. Cook sugar in water for 5 mins.. Add cranberries and orange, cook for 3 to 5 mins. Add 7 tbsp. apricot jam and lemon juice, stir, and cook for a few more minutes. Add almonds, and chill.

SWEET POTATO CRUNCH

This recipe was given to me by Grandma Sharon December of 2007 and, it quickly became a family favorite!

INGREDIENTS:

For the potato mixture:
6 boiled mashed sweet potatoes (boil them until the skin cracks, let them cool, take the skin off)
1 cup sugar
½ stick butter
½ cup milk
1 tsp cinnamon
2 eggs, yolks and whites beaten separately, with a fork or whisk
For the topping:
2 cups oats (the kind you use to make oatmeal)
1 cup dark brown sugar
1 cup nuts (I suggest walnuts or pecans), chopped
1 stick butter

INSTRUCTIONS:

In large mixing bowl which goes into a mixer, mix sweet potatoes, sugar, milk, ½ stick melted butter and cinnamon completely. Add beaten egg yolks. Mix completely, then fold in egg whites. Pour into a cooking dish (I use Corning Ware) and set aside.

For topping, melt one stick of butter and pour into a medium bowl. Add oats, dark brown sugar and nuts mixing well. Sprinkle this over the potato batter.

Bake 30-40 minutes at 350 degrees or until knife comes out clean when stuck into center.

PORT GLAZED TURKEY BREAST

I got this recipe when I took a Home Chef cooking class in San Francisco. It was part of a Light Holiday Menu. I really do love this recipe. And, you can use a whole turkey instead of a turkey breast.

INGREDIENTS:

1 Fresh Turkey Breast, about 6 lbs
2 onions, peeled and cut in half
6 cloves of garlic, crushed
2 carrots, cut into 4 pieces each
1 cup Port wine (use a decent wine)
1 cup chicken stock
1/2 cup water
1/2 cup honey
2 Tbsp. light soy sauce
Fine sea salt
Freshly ground black pepper

INSTRUCTIONS:

Place the turkey breast skin side up on a rack in a roasting pan. Place the onions, garlic and carrots around the turkey. Combine the port, stock, water, honey and soy sauce, and spoon the mixture over the turkey. Sprinkle the turkey with salt and pepper.

* * *

Roast the turkey in a pre-heated 400 degree oven for about 1 1/2 hours, until it tests done, basting it every 30 minutes. Replace the basing liquid with water or stock when necessary. Cover the turkey with foil and stop basting when the turkey turns a dark brown.

Remove the turkey from the pan and allow it to cool for 15 minutes before carving. Discard the vegetables remove the fat from the pan juices, and pour the pan juices into a saucepan, bring to a boil, and reduce to 1 cup of liquid. To remove the fat, I usually use a special cup that separates the fat from the other liquids. This will be your sauce/gravy.

Slice the turkey, arrange on a platter, and serve with the sauce. 230 calories and 1.5 grams of fat per serving, serves 8-10 people

MASHED POTATOES

These are the mashed potatoes that Grandma Sharon has made over the holidays for years.

INGREDIENTS:

1 baked potato per person plus a few extra, use white potatoes (Yukon gold is not a bad choice)
Salt , a few pinches
1 Tbsp. unsalted butter per potato
Milk (maximum of 4 oz.)

INSTRUCTIONS:

Peel the potatoes (with a potato peeler) an cut them in a uniform size. If you want to get the potatoes ready before the meal, just do this step early and keep the potatoes in cold, ice water to keep them from turning brown.

45 minutes before dinner, put the bowl of potatoes in water on the stovetop. Boil (on high heat) until they fork easily (abut 30 minutes). When just about ready for dinner, drain the water from the pan of potatoes and put the potatoes in the blender an start mashing. Add a little salt and about 1 Tbsp. Butter for each potato.Beat on high. Add milk (a little at a time) to make the mashed potatoes fluffy but not grey. Cover the mashed potatoes (to keep them warm) until ready for dinner.

GRANDMA SHARON'S STUFFING

This recipe is for the stuffing Grandma Sharon makes every year. Feel free to use vegetable broth instead of chicken bullion and water.

INGREDIENTS:

2-3 bags of Peppridge Farm Stuffing (it's getting hard to find. Use some kind of cube shaped dried bread and get as much as you need)_
Canned mushrooms (I use two small or one large can of good mushrooms or fresh mushrooms), drain out the fluids
1 egg, mix the white and yolk in a separate dish before adding
Melted butter (Melt 1 stick of butter and let it cool before adding)
Chicken boullion mixed with water per instructions (OR use Vegetable stock)
Chopped celery (I usually chop up about 3 sticks of celery)
Poultry seasoning (plan on using a whole spice container of poultry seasoning although just put in a little at a time until it tastes right)
Chopped onion (one big onion chopped up)

INSTRUCTIONS:

Put the stuffing mix, mushrooms, chopped celery

and chopped onion in a big bowl. Stir it up. Add butter and vegetable stock (or chicken boullion mixed with water) and the egg. Stir it up. Add more fluids as you see fit until it's moist but not too moist. You can add more butter (may be 1/2 a stick and/or more vegetable stock). Now, add a good amount of poultry seasoning (I'd say start out with 2 Tbsp.)…stir, taste. If it needs more poultry seating, just add more.

You can stuff the stuffing in the turkey before baking OR put the stuffing in a baking dish and cover and cook for about 30 minutes at 350 degrees.

Christmas Sugar Cookies

CHRISTMAS SUGAR COOKIES

This is a recipe from Grandma Sharon. We use cookie cutters to make the cookies in different shapes and frost artistically!

INGREDIENTS FOR BATTER:
1/2 cup Butter, softened
1 cup Sugar
1 Tbsp. Heavy Cream
1 Egg
1/2 tsp. vanilla
1 3/4 cup All Purpose Flour
1/2 tsp. Salt
1 tsp. Baking Powder

INGREDIENTS FOR FROSTING:
Powdered Sugar
Butter (softened)
Milk or Cream
Food Coloring

INSTRUCTIONS:

Cream butter (in a mixer), add sugar gradually, and add cream until light. Beat in egg and vanilla. Add dry ingredients (baking powder, salt, flour). Put the batter in the refrigerator for a few hours to chill.

Make about a cup of dough in a ball shape (go ahead, use your hands!). Roll with a rolling pin on a lightly floured board. Cut out with cookie cutters. Put the cookies on a cookie sheet (doesn't have to be greased). Bake at 350 degrees for 8 minutes.

Frost with a powdered sugar, butter and milk mixture. Add food coloring to get the colors you want. Do not use butter for the white colored frosting.

It also helps to have sprinkles, M&M's, and small chocolate chips on and to help with the decorating! Have fun!

After the frosting dries, you can put the cookies in a tin and keep them for awhile (may be a few weeks).

ZUCCHINI BREAD

This is the recipe Grandma Sharon used for years to make a delicious zucchini bread.

INGREDIENTS:

1 loaf pan (9 inches by 5 inches)
1 cup sugar
1/2 cup oil (I use Canola Oil, but I think Grandma uses Vegetable Oil)
2 eggs
1 1/2 tsp. Dried orange bits (if you can't find them, just skip them)
1 1/2 cup flour (use presifted flour)
2 tsp. Baking powder
1/2 tsp. Baking soda
1/2 tsp. Salt
1/8 tsp. Ginger
1/8 tsp. Mace or Nutmeg
1 cup grated Zucchini (I use a cuisinart but you can use a regular grater, keep the skin on, you can add more zucchini too and it'll just taste better)
1/2 cup chopped nuts (I like pecans or walnuts)
Powdered sugar

INSTRUCTIONS:

Spray the pan with cooking spray/oil or coat the pan with butter and pour flour on top of the spread out butter, shake, and pour out the flour that didn't stick to the butter. Preheat the oven to 375 degrees.

Beat the sugar, oil, eggs and orange bits together in a mixer until well blended. Add the dry ingredients and zucchini to the blended mixture and mix.

Stir in the nuts. Pour the mixture into the pan. Bake at 375 degrees for 55 minutes. Cool for 15 minutes and then sprinkle with powdered sugar. You can take the loaf out of the pan as soon as it's cool enough (I would try to take the loaf out of the pan before pouring some powdered sugar on top, but the powdered sugar needs to be sprinkled on when it's still warm on the top)

MEASUREMENTS AND EQUIVALENTS

a dash = 8 drops (liquid) ≈ ⅛ teaspoon (slightly less)

1 teaspoon = 60 drops

3 teaspoons = 1 tablespoon = ½ fluid ounce

½ tablespoon = 1½ teaspoons

2 tablespoons (liquid) = 1 fluid ounce = ⅛ cup

3 tablespoons = 1 ½ fluid ounces = 1 jigger

4 tablespoons = ¼ cup

⅛ cup = 2 tablespoons

⅙ cup = 2 tablespoons + 2 teaspoons

⅓ cup = 5 tablespoons + 1 teaspoon

1 cup = ½ pint = 8 fluid ounces

2 cups = 1 pint = 16 fluid ounces

4 cups = 1 quart = 2 pints = 32 fluid ounces

4 quarts = 1 gallon

* * *

1 peck = 8 quarts = 2 gallons

1 bushel = 4 pecks